Central Park

A PHOTOGRAPHIC EXCURSION

Library of Congress Cataloging-in-Publication Data

Freund, James C., 1934 –
        Central Park : a photographic excursion / James Freund.
        p. cm.
    ISBN 0-8232-2160-1 – ISBN 0-8232-2161-x (pbk)
    1. Central Park (New York, N.Y.) – Pictorial works.
    2. New York (N.Y.) – Pictorial works. I. Title.

F128.65.C3 F74 2001
974.7'1 – dc21
2001033465

Design by Bert Waggott

Printed in Italy

10 9 8 7 6 5 4 3 2 1

TITLE PAGE:
The montage on the title page is a detail from the poster used for the author's exhibition of Central Park photographs at the Arsenal Gallery in April 2000 (see pp. 140-1).

CONTENTS FACING PAGE:
The original version of this vignetted image of spring blossoms framing Cleopatra's Needle can be found on p. 99.

FRONT ENDPAPER:
This panoramic view, looking north, was taken from a vantage-point atop a tall building near the southeast corner of Central Park.

REAR ENDPAPER:
The ornate design of Ladies Pavilion on the Park's Hearnshead promontory is highlighted against the Central Park South skyline.

Central Park

A PHOTOGRAPHIC EXCURSION

James Freund

"Bethesda in Bloom"

"Plowing the South 40"

A PARK FOR ALL SEASONS

"C.P.W. Frosty"

"Sunday in the Park"

FORDHAM UNIVERSITY PRESS · NEW YORK · 2001

Contents

The Big Apple's Core

A bird's-eye view of Central Park looking north from a rooftop on 57th Street near Fifth Avenue.

1 🌿 Introduction

This book is my attempt to reflect the breadth of photographic possibilities afforded by Central Park.

We have this great treasure in our midst – a cornucopia of trees and rocks and quiet lanes. For cramped apartment dwellers, Central Park is literally our own backyard. It's not a private preserve, restricted to the wealthy or a social elite, nor is it a tourist haven shunned by locals; rather, it beckons all to roam its pathways and enjoy its beauty. And, in this priciest of cities, where most things cost an arm and a leg, this one is free.

The pleasures of the Park are manifold. Such diversity! It appeals to children and teenagers, to young adults as well as senior citizens. You can use it for exercise – to bike, skate, jog, row, play sports – for strolling or relaxation, for birdwatching or a visit to the zoo, to sunbathe or picnic, or just to appreciate its beauty and interest. The attractiveness of Central Park is unlimited: the blooming flora, the multiple fauna, the architecture, the waterways, the craggy rocks, the remarkable statuary – the list goes on and on. And all this against the kaleidoscopic background of the changing seasons – verdant spring, lush summer, colorful fall, and snowtipped winter. There's beauty and starkness, humor and pathos, activity and quietude 🌿 a little bit of everything.

Over the years, I've traveled quite a bit, in the U.S. and abroad, and have encountered some wonderful and interesting locales along the way. But as a New Yorker, I'm proud to say that I've never visited any single attraction that has more to offer the photographer than our own Central Park.

Up, Up, and Away

Here's the kind of enticing color vista you can capture with your camera – a massive rock, spring flowers, the shadows cast by the limbs and leafless branches of a shapely tree, a gazebo perched on high, and the Fifth Avenue skyline for a backdrop.

Heading Home

This is a poignant Park moment that black & white film captures so well. Note the rounded contours of both the woman and her canine companion, as they traverse the leafy carpet of late fall toward outstretched arboreal arms, with a traditional lamppost marking the venue.

I look upon Central Park and photography as kindred spirits. Just as the Park is available to all, so photography isn't mysterious or aloof or reserved for professionals, but has become the most accessible of the arts, open to everyone. And it matches the Park's diversity, offering multiple options in terms of subject matter – landscapes, people, still lifes, animals – while allowing the shutterbug to shoot in color or black & white, take stills or video, or (my own preference) do a little of each, since every medium has its own particular vitality and significance.

Reaching Out

Here are two snaps of the same scene, one in color and the other in black & white, illustrating some of the advantages of each medium (color for the solicitation, black & white for the acceptance!).

The Pretty Bichon

Family photographs work especially well in the Park when they incorporate some flavor of the local inhabitants. This is my family's dog, Lucy, as a pup, perched on Hans Christian Andersen's storybook. Note the ugly duckling's surrogate mother glaring up jealously from below.

New Yorkers who use the Park regularly will see a lot of familiar sights in these pages, but perhaps in a new light. For those Manhattanites who have been taking the Park for granted and missing out on such a treasure, I hope my book will serve as a reintroduction to this crown jewel set in the middle of the city. And for visitors to New York, Central Park is one of the best treats you're in for – don't miss it!

Winter *Spring*

The Four Seasons

In Central Park, every season is sheer delight.

Summer *Fall*

2 ✿ The Seasons of the Year

When you live in New York City and visit Central Park frequently, you're quite aware of its different "looks" as the seasons change. In fact, the title of the exhibition of my Central Park photographs at the Arsenal Gallery that formed the inspiration for this book (see pp. 140-1 and the title page) was "A Park for All Seasons". Photographers are quite cognizant of the prime times to take Park pictures. My personal favorites are when the buds come out in the spring (for both color and black & white shots), the glorious hues of autumn (in color), and the snows of winter (mostly in black & white). By the way, there's nothing wrong with the lush look of summer either.

An Icon for All Seasons

The iconic Park lamp is here wreathed by the forsythia of spring and the fading leaves of fall.

Rock Garden

Printemps Promenade

 *Spring*

For the color photographer, the buds and blossoms of spring are a special treat, whether capping a rock formation (facing page) or framing a woman, her dog, and the baronial reflection on still waters (above).

Spring Comes to
Strawberry Fields

Strawberry Fields is enchanting at all times of the year, but is at its finest in spring, sporting its profusion of blossoms, as shown in these two pictures. By the way, the reclining tree (right), is located just to the left of the one that's standing up tall (top).

The Buds of Bethesda

Black & white can also capture the magic of spring, as embodied in these buds reaching out to the silhouetted angel atop Bethesda Fountain.

Plowing the South 40

Summer is lush in the Park. I got a kick out of the rural-urban mix in this scene from the fields of Sheep Meadow.

Summer

**The Bridges of
New York County**

*The Park's
alluring
bridges,
such as
Gapstow
Bridge
(top)
and Bow
Bridge
(right),
attain scenic
heights
when
enveloped
in their
opulent
summer
attire.*

Fall

A Splash of Color

Autumn is all about color, as seen in the burnished gold of the Mall's dense foliage.

Heading South

A recurring September theme is the sight of migrant geese pausing on the banks of the Harlem Meer on their way south.

The Vestiges of Fall

I'm also attracted to the sparse – but still lustrous – leaves of November.

Hosting Halloween

The pumpkin fest that blankets Bethesda Terrace has become an annual October event.

15

Winter

A Cluster of Limbs

Snowy Silhouette

In winter, black & white photography takes over, especially on the heels of a snowfall. Having shed their leafy mantles, the branches of trees come alive against the stark white background (top), while other familiar Park shapes – rocks, the lakeside shelter, benches, ducks, even a litter basket – take on additional interest (left).

**After the
Storm**

**Icy
Aviary**

Some of the best winter shots
are of the big rock clusters
with their frosty topping,
modeled against the skyline
backdrop on a sunny day
after a snowstorm (top).
This was taken on the
promontory known as
Hearnshead which juts out
into the Lake in the west 70's.

When it's really cold, the
Lake freezes over and
provides a reflecting surface
for tree shadows as well as a
flight deck for the perennial
pigeons (left).

Misty

(See caption on facing page.)

Captured in the Crevices

**C. P. W.
Frosty**

Don't put away your color film in winter. You can get some subtle effects from a hazy landscape (facing page, top) and interesting patterns of snow on rocks (facing page, bottom). And if you're really lucky, there might be just a bit of pigment, as on the nose of Central Park West's lovable snowman (above).

Crossed Seasons

Only rarely are we fortunate enough to have the seasons overlap dramatically. Such a moment occurred on Sunday morning, April 9, 2000, when a freak spring snowstorm briefly blanketed the blossoms at Bethesda Fountain, Bow Bridge, and elsewhere. By late afternoon, the snow disappeared, and spring – slightly the worse for wear – resumed its visual hegemony.

(See caption on facing page.)

Some of the best people pictures are of young folks, especially kids. We tend to get bogged down taking snapshots of our own children and forget about all the other youngsters who scamper down slides, jump rope, dance around a fountain, or pick flowers. They're natural, unposed, and appear to be happy. This is the Park at its best.

Old Faithful

A fountain, however scenic, is just a fountain — that is, until a young girl happens by and is entranced by its effervescence, at which point it becomes a picture. Similarly, it's the resolute crew of landlubbers that animates this everyday rowboat scene (facing page).

3 ✤ People

Central Park may possess some glorious scenery but it's no wilderness. Rather, this is a landscape that's full of people – which, after all, is the reason for its being there. (Early proponents of the Park proclaimed that it would "serve as lungs for the city".) And, in terms of photography, human beings themselves are often the best subjects of all.

The activities they're engaged in may be strenuous, as in biking, skating, jogging – even cross-country skiing. Or there may be quieter pursuits, such as painting, playing music, fishing, boating, birdwatching, frolicking with a dog, or perhaps just relaxation and sunbathing. The photo opportunities are always present.

Three in a Row

Telemarker about Town

There are bikers, skaters, and joggers galore, but it's a special day when you spot a cross-country skier gliding across the Park.

Facing page:

Although fewer of them are visible nowadays than in generations past, a horse and rider on the Park's bridle path is always a welcome sight (top left).

The waters off Bethesda Terrace offer surprising opportunities to these young anglers (top right).

The Park also contains some ideal locales for tranquil undertakings (bottom).

On the Trail

Catch and Release

A Quiet Place

Black & white is an ideal medium to capture special moments, featuring the Park's many visitors.

Reading Robbie Burns?

Rummaging

Bridal Party

The Garrulous Cabbie

27

A Covey of Birdwatchers

Central Park also lends itself to group activities, such as birdwatching (top) and running (below). But what really fascinated me was the exercise routine of the young mothers (facing page, top), stretching and then jogging with some special cargo along for the ride.

In Full Stride

Mamathoners   *(See caption on facing page.)*

Master Class

*The Park vistas,
particularly from April
through October, are
appealing to artists,
either alone (left) or in
a group (top).*

Solo Effort

Duet

The Man with the Horn

Dig those Sounds

Good weather also brings out the musicians. Some perform in small combos on a commercial basis (top left and bottom), while others prefer the solitude of a woodsy site (top right).

Couples

These two pages are devoted to couples, including the mounted troopers on duty (left). This may be fanciful, but I see the other shots (although involving three different twosomes) as forming a continuum – first the courtship (top left), then the nuptials (facing page), and finally the rest of life with each partner doing his or her own thing (top right).

(See caption on facing page).

Youthful Frolics

(See caption on facing page.)

Double Dutch

Youth must be served — and the Park provides an ideal setting for just that, whether it's ersatz rock-climbing (facing page, top left), jumping rope (above), or, for the younger set (facing page), sliding, swimming, or hoola hooping.

(See caption on facing page.)

Tykes

The Park is a delight for children, whether hiding from daddy (facing page, top), petting the flowers (facing page, bottom), sharing a slide (top), or meeting a new friend (right).

Ursa Major

Here's Manhattan's most formidable resident in repose.

4 ✿ Animals

Central Park is chock full of animals. They come in basically three varieties: the denizens of the small but lively zoo; the free-roaming wildlife – squirrels, ducks, swans, and so forth; and the dogs and other domestic pets of Manhattan citizenry. All make potentially marvelous photographic subjects – if they'll just hold still long enough for you to get the shot.

You shouldn't underestimate the zoo. The polar bears are sublime, the penguins perky, there are monkeys to be reckoned with, and the sea lions put on quite a spectacle.

Taking the Sun

Mirroring his ursine colleague's downtime, this otherwise frisky sea lion is soaking up a few late-afternoon rays.

Gone Fishin'

Be sure to visit the zoo at feeding time. If you're lucky, you might get a snap of a sea lion opening wide to ingest a fish or two.

Black & White in Kodacolor™

These swans hang out at the zoo. I was particularly taken by their black and white pigments midst the autumnal setting.

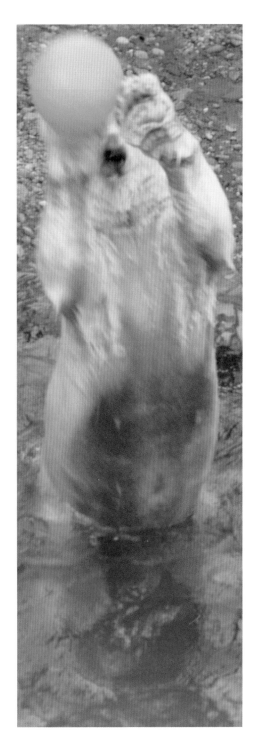

Hoops, Anyone?

*This Arctic crowd-pleaser, frolicking
with its latest plaything, is caught
in action, displaying some
Michael Jordan-like moves.*

Little Leaguers

The Park abounds with ducks (top left, plus a stray pigeon), but it's still gratifying to catch them maneuvering in formation (left). Squirrels (top right) are ubiquitous and, if they'll stick around for a moment, quite photogenic (see also pp. 89 and 98).

Deux Chevaux

As for equines, you have your choice of heroic steeds on a pedestal (with Simón Bolívar astride) and the more prosaic variety hitched to a carriage on Central Park South.

Hinterland Habitat

Turtles are far fewer in number, so it was quite fortuitous when this little guy popped up to claim his place in the scheme of things. (See also p. 96.)

Meanwhile Down in the Bulrushes

A graceful swan is at home in the bulrushes, with the turreted Beresford hovering on high.

En Famille

Here's mama swan venturing out with her cygnets.

Pooch Playground

As a dog owner, I realize how important the Park is for the otherwise penned-in canine citizens of Manhattan. So this page is dedicated to pooches – in pairs (top left) or forming a sextet (top right), dressed up (bottom right) or cast in bronze like Balto (bottom left), who led a sled team of huskies through a blizzard to deliver the serum that saved Nome.

Our lovable bichon, Lucy, who relishes her daily forays to the Park, would never forgive me if she didn't get her own page in this book. So here she is — staring down a great dane and playing hard-to-get with a persistent suitor.

Lucy in the Park with Doggies . . .

Central Canal

Call it hokey, but the sight of this gondolier (first cousin to the charioteers on pp. 60-1) near the Boathouse Café (facing page, top) is my kind of kitsch. And let's not forget the Park's landmark watering hole, Tavern on the Green (facing page, bottom).

5 ❦ Significant Others

This chapter contains a potpourri of additional worthwhile sights the Park has to offer – giant rocks, watery vistas, toy sailboats, reflections and silhouettes, glimpses of horse and carriage, Belvedere Castle and vicinity, Conservatory Garden, the remarkable Bethesda Fountain, some splendid statuary, eateries, and views from a high perch.

Boathouse Café

(See caption on facing page.)

Tavern on the Green

**Dairy
Products**

Speaking of Park eateries, consider these two less pricey alternative venues.

**Spring
Treats**

Along the Lake's Eastern Shore

Here are two views of the Lake from the Boathouse Café (top left and bottom). To be able to spot Bethesda Fountain (top right), you have to scramble atop a rock in the nearby Ramble.

"... And Not a Drop to Drink"

It's difficult to photograph the Reservoir from ground level because of the unrelenting chain-link fence surrounding it (top); but if you persist, you can find some chinks in the armor. Here's one view looking west (middle) and the other to the southeast (bottom).

Starboard Tack

The official name is Conservatory Water, but I've always thought of this body of water as the sailboat basin.

One area of the Park where I haven't spent nearly enough time, but can certainly recommend, is the northeast corner, featuring the Conservatory Garden and the Harlem Meer. As the pictures on these two pages and elsewhere attest (see, for instance, pp. 22, 93 and 131), this region is one of the most scenic (yet less well known) of the Park's many treasures. If your taste runs to flowers and shrubs, fountains and statuary, water and wildfowl, don't miss out on the gems it offers – and with far fewer people in your line of sight.

Harlem Meer

(See text above.)

Front Yard

**Follow
the
Leader**

(See text on facing page.)

**Ready . . .
Camera . . .
Action!**

Willow Weep for Me

(See caption on facing page.)

To my mind, the Park's most unexpected (and perhaps least appreciated) territory lies just above 100th Street, a short distance in from Central Park West. This area is so woodsy and rustic that it's hard to believe you're still in New York City – caverns and cascades, stunning stone arches, meandering streams, weeping willows, the works. I'm ashamed to say that, despite all the years I've lived in Manhattan, I just discovered it recently. But I expect to return many times.

Huddlestone Arch

Glen Span Arch

A View of the Falls

That's called the Pool (facing page, top left) with its weeping willows, ducks, and such. The magical waterfall (left) leads from the Pool and Glen Span Arch to the Loch. And then there's the remarkable Huddlestone Arch, constructed entirely of huge boulders fitted together, yet sturdy enough to hold the East Drive on its shoulders.

The Pool
in Summer

*The Pool in
the northwest
corner also
looks good in
black & white.*

Missing in Action

*But for the helmets, this scene
photographed in the same area
of the Park might have come
from a Hollywood western
featuring the U.S. cavalry.*

**The Ol'
Swimmin'
Hole**

*Central Park provides swimming (and skating in the winter) at Lasker Rink and Pool
(107th Street), as well as tennis; the courts are located just northwest of the Reservoir.*

**Passing
Shots**

(See caption on facing page.)

The Carriage Trade

A trademark sound in Central Park is the clip-clop of horses drawing carriages. They're quite a sight, too, especially when blending into the surroundings – spotted behind a blanket of spring blossoms, framed by a splash of forsythia, or circling the fountain atop Cherry Hill (facing page, top). Take a ride sometime on a delightful May afternoon.

There's an abundance of natural beauty in the Park – trees, lakes, groves, and so forth. For me, though, the most spectacular sights are the giant rock outcroppings that can be found in various locations and sometimes appear to dwarf the buildings in the background.

Bedrock Foundation

(See caption on facing page.)

Winter Coat

Here are two pictures of the same gigantic rock formation, taken in different seasons, with the towers of Central Park West in the low 70's furnishing the backdrop.

Silhouette Meets Shadow

In this picture, I like the interplay between the reflected trunk and limbs and the silhouetted branches — all emerging from the canvas of the iced-over lake.

In a Mist

The shadows from the trees are picked up in the spray of an early morning watering of Strawberry Fields.

Liquid Refreshments

The waters of Central Park are a delight for the photographer. In case you haven't noticed, one of my favorite venues is the Lake – shown here in the spring (top) and in the fall (left).

Here are two other watery treats nestled beneath towering skylines – the sailboat basin (see also p. 53) at East 74th Street (top) and the Pond just off Central Park South (right).

The View from Turtle Pond

Theatre in the Round

The battlements of Belvedere Castle (facing page) dominate the mid-Park area south of the Great Lawn. One of our 20th-century apartment house castles (the Beresford) looms above the terrace of the Belvedere (top left). The ground level view is from Turtle Pond (top right), while the panorama from the terrace features Delacorte Theatre (bottom left).

Latter Day Castles

Delacorte by Day

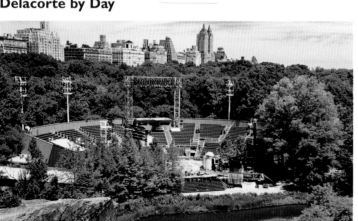

Castle in the Air

A view of the Castle, over Turtle Pond, early one summer morn.

Facing page, bottom right:

Numerous events — spontaneous or otherwise — occur within the confines of the Park. I never did find out what this happening was, although I think the shape of the structure provides a clue to its sponsorship.

The Park's remarkable statuary and monuments, which blend so effortlessly into the scenic design, are well worth savoring. Just look at the examples on the next few pages.

Daniel Webster

This is the renowned pre-Civil War senator and orator Daniel Webster – "Liberty and Union, Now and Forever, One and Inseparable" – from the front, from the rear, and up close and personal.

Ride to Glory

Here's one of the Park's most dramatic monuments – dedicated to José-Julian Marti, the apostle of Cuban independence – which is located near 59th Street and the Avenue of the Americas.

Significant Statuary

This page features The Indian Hunter (top left), The Falconer (top right), Christopher Columbus (bottom left), and the monument dedicated to the 7th Regiment (bottom right).

Forebears in Bloom

In springtime, I like to photograph statues in their colorful settings and then zoom in for a close-up. These monuments commemorate a Pilgrim Father (top) and Alexander Hamilton (bottom).

Virginal Verdigris

In terms of replicas of the fairer sex, you can't do better than this lovely maiden in the Conservatory Garden (top) or Lewis Carroll's Alice with her new friends (left), just north of the sailboat basin.

Wonderland

Ready to Pounce

One of the Park's covert treasures is located on the main eastside artery at the edge of the Ramble. The early morning exercisers (left) seem unaware of the predator lurking in the shadows atop the rocky outcropping (bottom).

Birds of a Feather

Fortunately, these pigeons taking a break above Simón Bolívar near Central Park South were on their best behavior the day I came upon the scene.

Ludwig von Brainwaves

Each time I walk near the Bandshell during winter, I envision the bare branches as neural waves emanating from Beethoven's sizable brain.

The Met

The vast Metropolitan Museum of Art takes up a hefty chunk of the Park along Fifth Avenue from 80th to 84th Streets. These pictures show the Met interacting with the Park – furnishing a backdrop for succulent blossoms (top) and reflecting the early spring landscape (right).

Bethesda Terrace and Fountain   *(See text on facing page.)*

If I had to select a single favorite place to take pictures in the Park, it would probably be Bethesda Fountain and its environs. Appearing on these four pages are various views in black & white (it also photographs well in color): through the arches from the arcade at the south end (facing page, top), and against the backdrop of the Lake (facing page, bottom); the Angel of the Waters in silhouette (right), high above the supporting structure (bottom); and, on the next two pages, the four cherubs enjoying a summer shower.

**Cherubs
Midst the
Cascade**

*(See text on
previous
page.)*

(See caption on facing page.)

The View from Overhead

These close-up shots were taken with a zoom lens from the roof of a skyscraper on 57th Street. That's the Metropolitan Museum and the Reservoir (facing page, top), the Hecksher Ball Fields (facing page, bottom), the Gapstow Bridge and pathway bordering the Pond in the southeast corner of the Park (top), and the Carousel (right).

November Neighbor

This panorama (left) of the Park in late November was taken from high up on a Central Park West terrace during Macy's Thanksgiving Day Parade.
I was also able to get a bird's-eye view of one of the big balloons (bottom) and an unusual angle on the shadow cast by a tree and gendarme (right).

Monkey-shines

What I like about this picture is that your eye is first drawn to the mammoth rock formation, then to the Fifth Avenue skyline in the background, and then — just when you're starting to wonder what this picture is really about — you spot the zoo's prize monkey poised on top of the rocks, dwarfed by his surroundings, but truly the focal point of the entire scene.

6 ✌ Tips on Photographing Central Park

In keeping with my theme of how accessible Central Park is to anyone with a camera, I've included this section as a primer on how to go about photographing the Park, in hopes that the reader will be encouraged to make the effort. Don't worry, I'm going to steer clear of technical stuff and jargon. This is just some common sense advice – illustrated by reference to specific photos – to those of you who otherwise reserve your cameras for travel or family snapshots.

Although I have abundant respect for professional photographers, one of the real virtues of photography is that it's not mysterious, grandiose, or aloof. The technology is so good nowadays that quite moderately-priced cameras can capture excellent images, while doing most of the work for you (focusing, adjusting exposure and speed). Just look at the picture below – shot with one of those $9 disposables!

Autumn in New York

The main concern for any photographer, professional or amateur, is to see the picture. You've all caught sight of these or similar scenes as you strolled or jogged through Central Park, but have you seen the *picture*?

Light and Shadow

It was a bright sundrenched day in the Park, but the subject matter at hand hardly seemed promising. Still, I managed to spot the picture. Do you see it?

Friends who observe me in action with a couple of cameras wrapped around my neck sometimes chide that I'm not really enjoying the scene – that I'm too busy snapping away. I respectfully disagree. I think that when I'm photographing, I scrutinize the surroundings more thoroughly than they do, and appreciate them more – plus I end up with a permanent record of what we both saw.

Squirreled Away

In the Arsenal show (see pp. 140-1), I displayed this as the final segment of a three-shot montage of the squirrel – first, up in the tree; then, landing on the picnic table to forage for food; and finally, two-thirds of the way inside the paper bag.

The Bullies on the Block

The Park pigeons and a few small ducks were enjoying a fine feast thanks to this caring citizen, when all of a sudden two big geese barged up to the front of the line.

Both the photographer and the casual observer begin by taking in the entire scene, letting it wash over them. But, for the photographer, that's usually just the starting point. Most good photos highlight some limited portion of the whole (a zoom lens is useful in this regard). With a camera, you're looking for shapes and forms, textures, relationships between objects and/or people, the interplay of light and shadow, and so on. This is often obscured in the overall setting, because it may be located in just one corner of the panorama. To spot it, you have to look at the scene with a photographer's eye. But hey – this isn't rocket science, it's not inscrutable, and anyone with a little imagination and patience can experience a real sense of satisfaction.

Easy Riders

The Bow Bridge and its surroundings offer prime photo opportunities. (See, for example, p. 121.) But on this particular day, I noticed an unusual sight on the bridge and zoomed in to capture the helmeted cowboy and his pardner astride trusty steeds. You don't need to see the rest of the bridge in this shot – you know it's there.

A Passing Phantom

I was quite fascinated by this spectral figure of a passing phantom, seemingly unnoticed by the jaded New York populace.

Out on a Limb

He's well camouflaged, but there's no mistaking this youngster climbing the diagonal tree limb. Note the iconic lamppost in the foreground, which firmly anchors the shot in Central Park.

92

Matching Pairs

What struck me here was the parallel between the classical youths adorning the fountain and the urban teenagers seated nearby – both duos just passing the time "hanging out."

Here *Cones* the Bride

A wedding is serious business, but, on this hot summer's day, in a corner of Bethesda Terrace, who could deny a little cool refreshment for the maid of honor?

Balls in the Air

Here's a special moment on Sheep Meadow, featuring a talented juggler and an admiring lad.

Now, the one prerequisite when you visit the Park is to have a camera with you, loaded with film and ready for use. You never know when you'll see something wonderful that has to be snapped at that moment or be lost forever.

For instance, one of my favorite shots is of a duck and a turtle perched on the same log, glaring at each other; I call it, *What the Hell Are* You *Lookin' At?* Unlike the professional wildlife photographer who waits in the bush for hours to get the shot, I just happened by with a camera in hand and saw the picture. A few minutes later, it would have been gone for sure. (I'll come back to this subject later in the discussion of photographing animals.)

What the Hell Are *You* Lookin' At?   *(See text above.)*

Bolder and Boulder

That's the famed Dakota serving as a Central Park West backdrop to these jumbo rocks.

When I want the viewer to know that the photo was taken in Central Park – hey, look at this magnificent boulder; it's not located out in the sticks somewhere, but right here in our urban midst – then I try to include something in the shot (a bit of skyline, a park icon perhaps) to mark it as such.

Snowy Coast

The Bow Bridge in the background plants this photo of small snowbound birds smack in the center of the Park.

So, for instance, the buds of spring are among the great delights of the Park, and you almost can't go wrong photographing them in any setting. But if you want to add some interest to the picture, as well as identify the scene as emanating from Central Park, then find some blossoms near a familiar landmark – as in the photo with Cleopatra's Needle (see facing page). But then, to emphasize that the picture is really about the flora, not the monument, you need to put the buds in focus and make the Needle blurry (although still readily identifiable). There's no great trick to this where, as here, the blossoms are much closer to the camera than the monument is. Just make sure the camera's autofocus is aimed at the flora, and the lens will do the rest for you – especially at larger apertures and/or longer focal lengths.

Little Fella

The fact that the squirrel is in sharp focus, while the large gazebo is not, makes the former stand out much more distinctly than if everything in the picture had been equally in focus.

Threading the Needle *(See text on facing page.)*

A Matter of Focus

In these two shots, I would have liked both the big cat and the fall foliage to be in sharp focus, but it couldn't be done because their relative distances from the lens were so divergent. I might have opted for a typical compromise, ending up with neither object totally sharp but not too blurry either. Instead, I decided to go for broke — with the result that the top photo has clear flora but fuzzy fauna, and the bottom just the reverse. They were framed together for the Arsenal exhibit to make the point.

Quite often, however, you would prefer all sections of the picture to be in clear focus, as in the four samples on the facing page. To accomplish this, it helps to select the smallest possible aperture for the lens (assuming you have such a choice) and then to aim at a point a little beyond the nearest of the important objects.

Spring Fever   *(See text on facing page.)*

An Afternoon Outing

October Aquatics

Harbinger of Spring

I like to juxtapose two or more themes that tell a story, make a point, or present an ironic contrast. The main subjects are often roughly equal in prominence, but they need not be — especially where the story line focuses principally on one of them. That's the case in the pictures on this page.

Cart and Strollers

The top image highlights the sleeping man beside his full shopping cart, with the tots in their strollers (figuratively, baby-carts) taking a back seat. In the bottom shot, the main emphasis is on the woman jogging with her dogs, while the man reclining on the outlying rock takes it nice and easy.

Exercise and Relaxation

Young Swingers

To show young people at play in the Park, you can either zero in on them (right) ...

... or silhouette them from a distance against the scenery and skyline (left).

Makeshift Gridiron

I often like to place within a single frame more than one photo, especially when the several images present an interesting contrast or reflect different aspects of the subject matter. (There's more discussion of this later, in terms of photo montages.) This can be especially effective in Central Park when you photograph the same scene in two different seasons. The pair on this page well illustrates this – the Pond and bridge at the southeast corner of the Park, bare and empty in winter, and then chock full of greenery and wildlife in mid-summer.

**Pond Scene
in Winter ...**

(See text above.)

**... And Six
Months Later**

Arches

There's a marked similarity in these two photos of arched limbs — until you look closer and realize that in the top shot those are spring buds partially obscuring the branches, while in the bottom a capping of snow performs the corresponding function.

A Day at the Beach

This rock-rimmed greensward is one of the spots in the Park where Manhattanites go to soak up a few rays of the sun ...

... but it's the patch of graffiti high on the rocks, that lends special character to the same locale.

Stone Age

Quite often you come upon a vista that presents an interesting wide-angle shot but also contains a segment that has something to offer by way of a close-up. When that happens, and if you have a zoom lens on your camera, then shoot it both ways.

Wintry Landscape

The two photos on this page offer a good example of this. The wide angle shot provides the perspective and traces the footprints on the frozen Lake, while the close-up reveals the pigeons and other features of the shoreline.

Everyday Park sights become a lot more photogenic if you come up with new ways to look at them. In that vein, don't be satisfied with the first shot you take of a desirable subject matter. That first glimpse is usually pretty straightforward – the way you see the subject as you happen upon it. Check if there might not be other, more imaginative ways to capture the image. Experiment, for instance, by including more or less of the scene, by moving around to shoot it from a different angle, or by elevating or lowering your point of view (if possible). You'd be surprised how often you can improve upon your original effort.

Slushy Seating

To illustrate the point, here are four pictures of the benches on the Mall, which are discussed on the facing page.

The Bench and the Bandshell

The first picture (facing page, top) is straightforward — not bad, but relatively uninteresting.

The second (facing page, bottom) is a close-up from a low angle that shows the sinuous curve of the corner bench with the Bandshell in the background.

The third (this page, top), which was taken from atop a nearby hill, displays the geometric pattern of the benches — something that can't be fully appreciated from ground level.

And the fourth (this page, bottom) is an unusual view of the benches from their back sides.

These latter three photos represent different approaches, all of which are more interesting than the head-on shot you see when you first come on the scene.

Patterns   **Backbenchers**

109

As a photographer your eyes have to be open for the unusual sight. In Central Park, there's enough going on for that to occur with some regularity. As you might expect, these happenings generally involve people – city dwellers who look a little different or who act in offbeat ways within the bucolic confines of their communal backyard.

So I was pleased, but not really that surprised, on the day when I happened upon this happy couple (bottom and facing page), just married, in formal dress except for their roller skates, taking their first waltz under the watchful gaze of the local citizenry.

Wedlock on Wheels   *(See text on facing page.)*

A Reservoir Runs Through It

I got a big kick out of this fly fisherman casting into his urban lagoon.

The Long Fetlock of the Law

For those city passengers not always enamored of our medallioned drivers, take heart in this image of a mounted policewoman ticketing the hapless cabbie.

Almost There

What particularly struck me here was the congruence between the angles of the man's crutches and the tree trunks in the background.

My Park, Too

The Park also serves as an occasional refuge for the less fortunate.

Synchronized Diving

People have asked me whether this is a photo of a statue. The answer is no – it's just a pair of frisky sea lions poised to plunge into their pool below – and with a bonus of the Plaza Hotel as a backdrop. (More sea lion photos can be found on pp. 39 and 40.)

When you're on the prowl for unusual Park sights, don't ignore the splendid little zoo located right behind the Arsenal near 64th Street and Fifth Avenue. It doesn't try to be comprehensive, but the exhibits it has are choice – and they can provide some superior animal images.

Bearish Backstroke

It's fascinating to watch this huge polar bear, effortlessly backstroking in its private pool (see also p. 41).

A Winter's Day

This picture and the one on the facing page – each taken from the same locale at the same time – illustrate how similar scenes can produce worthwhile photographs in both black & white and color.

Most of you are probably more familiar with color photography than with black & white, but you ought to consider trying the latter. Central Park lends itself particularly well to both modes. When I go out to shoot pictures, I invariably take along two cameras, one with each kind of film. Some photos need color (for example, to highlight the hues of autumn), some cry out for black & white (those winter snow/tree/rock scenes), and others look so good both ways that I shoot with both barrels. With regard to people, my rule of thumb is: the grittier the scene (the homeless man on p. 113, the couple at the Lennon Memorial on p. 123), the better black & white conveys the message; whereas, if you're trying to generate some warmth (the newlyweds on pp. 33 and 110-1, the father and son on p. 55), color captures the glow of the moment.

After the Storm

(See caption on facing page.)

By the way, I sometimes use a video camera to record images of Central Park, especially when there is motion involved (such as skaters), but also when I want to "tell a story" through a sequential montage of meaningful shots. I edited a number of such images onto a 50-minute videotape for the Arsenal show (see pp. 140-1), but unfortunately it can't be replicated between these covers.

Every year there are a few dozen great days in New York, when the air is clear and the sun sparkles; and if you have any choice in the matter, try to get out to the Park. Everything looks better and more inviting, and your pictures will have an extra dash to them.

Surreys with the Fall Fringe on Top

I am fascinated by the horse-drawn carriages, gamboling through the Park during fine weather, as here under the foliage of autumn.

Vertical New York

The brightness of the day serves to emphasize the soaring skyscrapers that frame Wollman Rink and are reflected in its icy surface.

Sun Worship

When winter recedes and spring arrives, a tanning session is very much in order.

Pot o' Gold

You may be lucky enough (as I was here) to capture a rainbow in the spray of the fountain, which occurred just at the same time as a couple of animated youngsters happened by.

*A polarizing
filter reduced
the glare
from the lake
enough to
permit me to
capture this
autumnal
overview of
the Park from
an open
apartment
window high
above Central
Park West.*

On the other hand, bright sunlight can also create some problems for the photographer. Frequently, if you're shooting a body of water, it may sparkle too much. This can often be cured by using a polarizing filter. Another difficulty occurs when the contrast between the sunlit and the dark portions of a picture is too much for the lens to handle (so that one part is washed out and the other too murky). At least with negative film, though, these problems can be ameliorated in the darkroom – if not in those one-hour prints from a machine.

As for people, sunlight can produce intense shadows on a subject's face which create unflattering effects. I find it preferable to take portraits of people in open shade, or with the sun behind them and using a fill-in flash, in order to expose their features to best advantage.

Bow Bridge in the Afternoon

A strong late afternoon sun bounces off Bow Bridge in the shot above, producing excess intensity. The glow is better balanced in the more subdued light suffusing the picture below.

Bethesda in Bloom

Notice how rich these blossoms near Bethesda Fountain look on a hazy spring day.

But, in any case, don't feel limited to shooting on sunny days. Big splashy scenes might look better with all that light and shadow, but if you narrow your focus, you can get good results on even the grayest of days. A friend of mine, who specializes in photographing gardens and flowers, told me that many of her best shots are taken on overcast days, with the soft light producing more intense colors. (See the discussion of *Sunday in the Park* on p. 143.)

Almost all sections of the Park contain interesting images, and I encourage you to explore its totality. I've made an effort to include photos from as many areas as possible, but I confess to a certain imbalance. The majority of my pictures are from (or look toward) the western and central portions of the Park – often with Central Park West or sometimes Central Park South in the background – bounded by the cross-streets of the 60's and 70's. That's because I invariably enter the park at 72nd Street and Central Park West – near my home – and start snapping right away! And on many of my excursions, I just don't have time to range too far afield. But I'm not apologizing for this, because many of the most interesting Park locales – Strawberry Fields, the Lake, Bethesda Fountain and Terrace, the Mall, and so forth – are in this area; and I've always considered the skylines of Central Park West and 59th Street to be the most photogenic.

Imagine All the People …

Strawberry Fields has an evocative memorial to John Lennon, who was shot and killed in front of the nearby Dakota. His admirers from around the globe come to visit and pay tribute.

Here's the best advice I can offer with regard to photographing people. When the individuals involved are the principal focus of the picture, make sure to include enough of them in the image to capture the viewer's attention. I would venture that the primary mistake amateur photographers make in this regard is that they don't get close enough – there's too much else in the scene that's competing for attention with the smallish individual figures.

For some professional lensmen, the issue of "getting up close" is solved only by doing just that – getting right in the subject's face with a wide angle lens. There's no question this introduces a sense of immediacy. Other photographers, however (and I include myself in this latter category), are a little shy about doing this – and, in New York especially, there may also be an element of danger, or at least embarrassment, involved. So, if you're like me, you stand a distance away using a zoom lens, extended to its telescopic extreme, to bring the individual into the forefront of the picture. An advantage of this technique, I find, is that the subject – usually unaware that his or her photo is being taken – has a more natural expression and posture than those who have just had a camera thrust in their faces.

Meditation

**The
Strenuous
Life**

(See text on facing page.)

**Green
Alleys**

Yellowjacket

In these two pictures, the main thrust is the scrumptious fall foliage that the Park offers every autumn. But each photo is made more interesting by the inclusion of people – the woman in the yellow windbreaker (reflected in the water) on this page and the scampering youngster on the facing page – even though they take up only a small fraction of the overall composition.

Fall Frolic   *(See caption on facing page.)*

The small animals and waterfowl that inhabit the Park can be fine subjects. When you happen on them in an attractive setting, my advice is to snap the picture immediately. Don't pause to adjust your camera, search for the best angle or superior light, or worry about how far to zoom in or out. There's plenty of time to do that on your second, third, and fourth shots. The thing to remember here (the case of birds being particularly in point) is that these creatures aren't rooted to the ground like a bush or a park bench; and while you're fooling around playing Ansel Adams, they may have bolted for other parts. So grab that first imperfect shot – it may be all you're left with, but that's better than nothing.

Up a Tree

I can think of a dozen other ways I might have wanted to capture this shot, but I had just a few seconds during which both the squirrel and my dog Lucy obliged – so I'm glad I let 'er rip.

Ducks in a Row

You can bet that these multiple ducks on a tree limb over the water weren't going to stick around for very long after I managed to get this shot.

Most good photographers today stress the need to take a lot more images than what they ultimately display. It comes with the territory. So don't be disappointed if only six of your 24 shots on the roll are worth keeping; be happy you got that many. Put the other 18 in the drawer and forget about them. My motto is shoot more and select less. And for those of you who take video, the same is true in spades. Keep the camera rolling, by all means; you never know when something memorable is about to happen. But then edit out all the stuff that doesn't make the grade or is merely repetitive.

So now you have some good images – what do you do with them? Or you have some prints you like, but perhaps one part of the composition is too light, and another too dark, or there are some extraneous objects within the picture.

I tip my hat to the one-hour photofinishers that abound nowadays. They do a fine job of producing usable 4 x 6 inch snapshot prints. For special pictures, however, you've got to take the next step, which is a custom enlargement. *Enlargement* because almost every picture (and particularly those in black & white) looks better in a larger format. *Custom* because a good photofinisher can usually improve your image – by lightening or darkening portions of the print, by the use of filters and the right paper to give the picture the proper tonality, by cropping to exclude extraneous elements, and so forth. It costs a few bucks, but compared to a lot of other things in life (especially around New York), this is really a bargain.

Just a word about cropping – selecting the portion of the scene that you want to emphasize. You can accomplish this at one or more of three different junctures. First, when you compose the picture in the viewfinder, especially if you have a zoom lens – but even without one if you move in closer to the subject. Second, when you tell the photofinisher how much of the negative you want enlarged. And third, with a paper cutter, if what emerges from the darkroom contains some obtrusive elements. But crop you must – to focus attention on what's significant and to eliminate some unwelcome intruders from your product.

His Master's Voice

You can see how much more impact this shot of dog, dog-owner and guitar has when extraneous elements are eliminated through cropping.

On the other hand, some "intruders" can be a most welcome sight for the photographer . . .

The Almost-Barefoot Contessas

Note the socks with which someone adorned two of the Three Dancing Maidens in the Conservatory Garden.

Two's Company

Can you distinguish the real bird from its brethren in bronze?

The reflections of objects in water often produce interesting images. The multiple bodies of water contained in Central Park offer the photographer plenty of locales to take full advantage of these opportunities.

Reflected in the Meer

The Harlem Meer provides a choice reflective surface for the twin spires of Schomburg Plaza (left) and the Charles A. Dana Discovery Center (bottom).

Below the San Remo Below the San Remo   *(See text on facing page.)*

Thirty-five mm film enlarges quite well – a sharp negative can easily go up to a 16 x 20 which is good for framing your best shots. For a free-standing framed photograph, 11 x 14 is about the smallest dimension that makes sense. Yet, I often have the photofinisher start by making an 8 x 10 or 8 x 12 print, which is the size of the black & white prints I work with in my darkroom.

The reason for this is that I'm a great believer in the montage technique for amateur photographers like you and me. Sure, if you take a fantastic picture, by all means blow it up big and frame it separately. But most of the better photographs we take aren't *that* good. Moreover, a single picture rarely tells the whole story of what I want to express – the look of a certain place, the image of adolescence, a variety of activities, or the essence of a season. So I create montages by assembling within a single frame anywhere from two to a dozen photos that, taken together, reflect almost prismatically the various facets of a subject, in order to convey its full flavor. And for this purpose, the smaller print works just fine. I included a large number of these montages in the Arsenal show, and I've composed two of them on the following pages to illustrate the point.

Central Park: Clicked in the Bud (pp. 136-7)

The subject matter here is floral – flowers, buds, and blossoms – in different shapes, sizes, and settings. (In the backgrounds, you'll recognize the Metropolitan Museum, the Shakespeare Garden, the lawn for bowling, Bethesda Fountain, the Conservatory Garden, and other points of interest.) It gives the viewer a good taste of what's available in the Park.

A Park for Strollers

*Here's a tribute to the walkways of the Park —
from steps framed by rustic handrails, to an ornamental
staircase; from an arboreal lane, to one meandering
below the 59th Street skyline.*

Central Park: Clicked in the Bud

(See footnote on page 134.)

✿ On a Personal Note

Taking these pictures and creating this book has been a
real labor of love for me. You see, I'm not a photographer by profession –
strictly an amateur shutterbug.

My career has been spent as a business lawyer, a partner in the large
law firm of Skadden, Arps, Slate, Meagher & Flom, primarily engaged in
handling mergers & acquisitions plus other corporate matters, as well as dispute
resolution (including acting as mediator and arbitrator). I also teach
and have written a number of books and articles on mergers, negotiating,
mediation, lawyering, etc.

But I've always pursued hobbies assiduously. Until recent years, my
primary leisure time activity was playing the piano in the jazz/popular/showtune
idioms. Then photography came into my life, ultimately attaining equal stature.
The two pastimes complement each other quite well, alternating the focus
between the eye and the ear. Since I retired from active legal practice a few years
ago, I've been able to give these pursuits a lot more of my time.

I don't recall taking photos as a youngster, or even in college,
although I did make some home movies of a cross-country trip during the
summer after graduation from high school. Following college in the '50s I
served aboard a Navy icebreaker, bought a camera, and photographed the
icebergs and penguins of Antarctica, the rugged charm of ports of call in New
Zealand, and such. But in the years after the Navy, except for a few vacations, I
put away my camera for law school and the early years of legal practice.

I picked up the camera again in the late '60s when my kids were
born. But my pictures were mainly of them, with less attention paid to their

surroundings. By the '80s, however, although my law practice kept me quite busy, I gradually began to comprehend what else could be accomplished with a camera – moving from family snapshots to photographing scenes typically connected with travel.

Having grown up as a city boy, I was accustomed to a world of concrete and glass. But when my wife (real estate broker/executive Barbara Fox) and I bought a house in Easton, Connecticut in the mid-'80s, my eyes were opened wide to the joys of nature. I became fascinated by the trees, the foliage, the quiet lanes, the change of season, the play of light and shadow. And I began to experiment with black & white film. I entered my work each year in a local photography contest and was pleased to receive some recognition. In 1997, there was a show of my pictures at the Easton Library.

When we made some renovations to our house in 1995, I put in a darkroom. Since then, I've spent some delightful hours in there, printing mainly 8 x 10 black & white images. (I still go to photo labs for larger prints and all color pictures.) In today's world of computers and other advanced technology (a world I've had difficulty confronting), I cherish the workaday low-tech atmosphere of a traditional darkroom. The chemistry is old stuff; the variables – such as lens opening and exposure time – are all straightforward. It could be 50 years ago, and I would have been doing essentially the same thing. (To emphasize these roots, I usually play Glenn Miller and Tommy Dorsey recordings on my cassette deck while printing.) I find the darkroom to be a real refuge.

But my heart is still in New York City, where we live only a half block away from Central Park. Since retirement, no matter what I've planned for any particular day, if the morning light is sparkling and I know there are buds on the trees or snow on the ground – or even when there's nothing special going on – I'll grab my cameras and head out to the park for a few choice hours. It's invariably a fresh and fulfilling experience.

Over the years, I had accumulated quite a few pictures of Central Park. Then in April-May 2000, I exhibited the best 225 of them in a show entitled "A Park for All Seasons," presented by the Parks Department of the City of New York, at the Arsenal Gallery adjacent to the Commissioner's office.

The Arsenal

The Arsenal, where my show took place, is the building with the round turrets in the bird's-eye view (left); that's part of the zoo adjacent to it. The entrance to the Arsenal's walkway is on Fifth Avenue at 64th Street. Note that the handrail struts are in the shape of muskets which, together with the cannonball triangles over the doorway, hark back to the building's former incarnation. The chandelier illuminates the Arsenal's ground floor lobby.

N.B.: All the pictures in this book, most of which were displayed at the show, were taken by me except for the shots of the Reservoir and tennis courts, pp. 52 and 59, bottom (Cyrus Moshaver); the Arsenal Gallery reception, p. 141 (Keyman Lew); and the still from the NY1 television feature, p. 141.

The Opening Reception, April 5, 2000

Here are some pictures from the opening reception of the Arsenal Gallery photo exhibition. At the top right, New York City Parks Commissioner Henry J. Stern (left) joins me. NY 1, the cable network, broadcast a special feature on the show just before the opening (middle left). Those are family members flanking me at the bottom left: sister-in-law, Marjorie Hilton; wife, Barbara Fox; son, Tom Freund; and mother, Marcy Freund.

Scenes from the Arsenal Gallery

This book is not intended as a guidebook to Central Park. I've made no attempt to provide history, or draw maps, or be comprehensive. Such books are available, however, and they can be quite rewarding; a good example is *Barnes & Noble Complete Illustrated Map and Guidebook to Central Park*.

Many people have helped me in these endeavors. For the Arsenal show, I want to express my appreciation to New York City's Commissioner of Parks, Henry Stern, and his colleagues Jonathan Kuhn and Caroline Edmunds, for making the exhibit possible; to Mark and Fima Lieberman (plus support from Albert Rodriguez) at Studio 72 Photography for the consistent excellence of their prints, and also to Modernage, which printed many of the earlier shots; and to Roz Strizver, Kay DeVorshock, and Richard Kuchta of Frame & Save in Easton, Connecticut for their superior skills in matting and framing. As for the book, my thanks to Bert Waggott and his colleague Rosemary Bella, talented graphic designers who did so much to shape the appearance of these pages; to Charles Davey, for expertly shepherding the book through its production and printing; to Saverio Procario and his colleagues at Fordham University Press, and especially Dr. Mary Beatrice Schulte for her astute editorial suggestions; and to my indispensable secretary, Ann Leyden, who took care of so many pesky details.

A special word of thanks to my good friend Cyrus Moshaver, who has been indispensable in coping with almost every aspect of the exhibit and this book, whose substantive contributions have been plentiful, and whose infectious enthusiasm for both projects has consistently buoyed my spirits.

In addition to the City's Parks Department and its indefatigable commissioner, all New Yorkers owe a resounding vote of thanks to the privately funded Central Park Conservancy, whose efforts in restoring, renovating, and maintaining our precious Park have been exemplary.

Let me also acknowledge my wife, Barbara Fox, for putting up with my "just one more shot" for so many years; my mother, Marcy Freund; and my sons, Erik and Tom. Thanks for your continued support.

And for those of you who joined me on this photographic excursion, I hope you enjoyed the trip.

May 2001   JIM FREUND

POSTSCRIPT

Sunday in the Park

This was the consensus favorite photograph of those who attended the Arsenal exhibit. I received numerous comments as to its "painterly" quality, its Seurat-like aspects, and so on. I wish I could say that I set out to create just such an image, but I can't remember doing so. In fact, I think it was simply serendipitous. This does illustrate, though, that you don't need to wait for bright days to go out shooting. The muted greens and browns that came into their own on this drab day created a mood that was ultimately more appealing than the splashiest sun-drenched autumn colors.

Incidentally, it turns out that *Sunday in the Park* has a mind of its own . . . After observing its features in the mirror one day, my pet photograph up and decided to reverse itself in order to put its best face forward on the front of the book's wraparound cover!